BEYOND

BEYOND

BEYOND

BEYOND

BEYOND

BEYOND

The Morrow of Life

Includes
A Course in Renaissance English

Original Manuscript by
Shillaber Montabue
1599

Edited by
Robert A. Steiner

Wide-Awake Books
Box 659, El Cerrito
California 94530

Beyond Beyond Beyond. © 1990 by Robert A. Steiner. All rights reserved. No part of this book may be reproduced in any manner whatsoever without written permission of Robert A. Steiner, except in the case of brief quotations. Inquiries should be addressed to Wide-Awake Books, Box 659, El Cerrito, California 94530

First Edition this century.

99 98 97 96 95 94 93 92 91 90   10 9 8 7 6 5 4 3 2 1

Library of Congress Catalog Card Number: 90-71012

ISBN 0-9623473-1-0

Manufactured in the United States of America,
a country worth saving.

To Wallace I. Sampson, M.D.

For his enormous insight, wisdom, friendship,
and,
in a very real sense,
for making this book, and many more things, possible.

Contents

THANK YOU!

Thank you, across the centuries, back to 1599, to Dr. Shillaber Montabue, for his brilliance and his inspiration. His writing was a sine qua non to this work.

Jim Letchworth was my original guide to the world of Renaissance England.

I was fortunate to be able to combine the wisdom of the sixteenth century with the technical production expertise of the eve of the twenty-first century.

Kent Harker, a production consultant and computer whiz, turned computer disks into an author's dream.

Bart Brodsky, a skilled graphics designer and renowned educator, assisted by Geoffrey Graham, designed the wondrous cover.

Whitehall Company did an excellent job in printing and binding. (This is being written before their work has even begun. However, there are those who believe that I can see into the future.)

The brass sculpture of the unicorn, by Hans Reisinger, Augsburg, 1589, is pictured on the cover with the kind permission of Richard Huber: *Treasury of Fantastic and Mythological Creatures;* New York: Dover Publications, Inc., 1981.

FOREWORD

The original manuscript of *BEYOND BEYOND BE-YOND*, by Shillaber Montabue, was published in 1599, in Oxfordshire, England.

Dr. Shillaber Montabue was a Professor of Philosophy, a Physician (Phisition), and a Scientist. He was an extraordinary educator, writer, and public speaker. He earned his livelihood by teaching and lecturing at universities, and by selling his manuscripts. He was a rarity: a free-lance itinerant professor, and a physician who did not practice medicine.

His home was all of England. He traveled from university to university, and from shire to shire.

Many considered Dr. Montabue to be a creative genius, with an understanding of life that was well ahead of his contemporaries. Virtually all agreed that he was a brilliant thinker; that was true even of those who disagreed strongly with his views.

Dr. Montabue first gained worldwide fame, in a matter of dubious distinction, at the age of 21. A student at Oxford University, his scholarship and popularity were both very high.

His philosophy professor was very upset at seeing that the majority of the students believed in mystical nonsense. She decided to play a hoax on the entire University, and requested Montabue's assistance. She correctly reasoned that he would be expert at the function. She knew that he had studied under Reginald Scot (author of *The Discoverie of Witchcraft*, 1584. Although *Discoverie* had not yet been published, Scot's scholarship and expertise in deception were well known in academic circles.).

The hoax was so successful that students and professors alike, as well as the general public, believed the fakery to be true. The new, *false* "wisdom" was soon accepted and believed worldwide, by millions of people.

With some considerable degree of pride, and with some slight embarrassment, the professor revealed the entire hoax exactly one year after it was perpetrated.

Most people were good sports about accepting the exposé, many learned the lesson to be a bit more skeptical about unsubstantiated claims, and a few were angry.

Montabue's role as secret assistant received only fleeting recognition. With the magnitude of the hoax, plus the startling realization that a woman had actually become a professor of philosophy at the prestigious Oxford University, Montabue's silent assistance faded into insignificance. Chroniclers throughout the world reported the entire incident in depth. Then, almost as an afterthought, some wrote: "She was assisted by a student named Shillaber." The majority missed even that explanation, and merely reported: "She was assisted by a shillaber."

Without the capital "s," Montabue's identity was totally absent from the story. The word *shillaber* entered our language to mean "secret assistant in a hoax." It was very quickly expanded to include secret accomplices in all sorts of nefarious transactions, including confidence games, cheating in gambling, and various criminal activities.

In time, as the language changed, *shillaber* was shortened to *shill*. It retains the broad meaning of virtually any secret accomplice.

The word *shillaber* followed Dr. Shillaber Montabue all of his life, used primarily by friends and associates to poke fun at him. He took it in quite good humor. After all, how many of us have had our names become words?

Dr. Shillaber Montabue virtually discovered and did precisely define the scientific method. Although he did not use the words *scientific method* (that term came into our language later), the concept was understood and practiced by him in his research.

His interpretations of *why* things happen were sometimes in error, *as viewed from our vantage point of several centuries later*. However, for his time, they were extremely good.

His methods of observation, inductive reasoning, formulation of hypotheses, scientific testing, and deductive reasoning were absolutely astonishing. Although he did not always know the *why* of occurrences, his observations and correct articulation of *what* was happening were virtually always right on target. You will find his explanations and insight to be remarkably critical and precise for a sixteenth century scholar.

Enough! Read his words. He says it far better than I can.

Robert A. Steiner

———————————

To learn to read, pronounce, and speak Renaissance English, please see A Course in Renaissance English in the back of the book.

BEYOND

BEYOND

BEYOND

The Morrow of Life

By

Shillaber Montabue

The manie manuscripts in this booke were writ by me o'er the course of mine owne education and my career as an educator of others.

Maihap I shall be fortunate enough to cause ye, my readers, to thinke anew on the ideas which I humblie present.

Prithee write to me, ech of ye, in care of the publisher, an thou hast anie comments, suggestions, dubiosities, or questions.

Thank ye for your scholarship.

Cleare Bookes
Oxfordshire
1599

This booke is dedicated to

Reginald Scot,

excellent freend,

extraordinarie philosopher,

and

courageous exposer of cousenage and absurditie.

The thanks I owe to Reginald Scot for his wisedome, encouragement, inspiration, freendship, as well as his kinde reviewe of my manuscripts o'er the years, are beyond what I can expresse.

INTRODUCTION

Thinke larger than a colossus.

Thinke deeper than the centre of Earth.

Thinke farther than the farthest starre.

Thinke greater than the universe.

Thinke anew of incredible.

Thinke more than infinitie.

Thinke beyond beyond.

Then, an thou art brave . . . an thou wilt allow thy minde complete freedome . . . then, and onelie then . . . *maihap* . . . shalt thou be able to explore beyond beyond beyond.

Venture thither with me.

PART I

BEYOND

Chapter 1

Welcome to
BEYOND BEYOND BEYOND

Is Earth flat? Nay, 'tis not. How knowe we that? Bicause, whilst moste folke throughout the world beleeved 'twas flat, a few brave souls set saile into unknowne waters. Manie, e'en moste, who knew of the venture issued the direst of predictions of the deathe of the courageous folke who dared to explore: "They will fall off the edge of Earth."

As we now knowe, they did not fall off the edge of Earth. Nay, indeede. These bold citizens of planet Earth discovered new lands, new waters, new people, new continents, new languages, &c.

They accomplished all of that bicause they dared to goe beyond where moste thought was the verie end of Earth . . . beyond the last frontier . . . beyond all knowne life.

❋ ❋ ❋ ❋ ❋ ❋

Is Earth the centre of the universe? Nay, 'tis not. Are we sure? Aye, we are sure. How can we be sure? Bicause a few, verie few, applied science to the studie of that verie question. They used logick, theorie, and empiricall observations. Then they did thinke on it throughlie.

Albeit 'twas considered by manie to be blasphemie, those daring philosophers and students of science spake publicklie. They went beyond where others dared to goe . . . beyond what others dared e'en to thinke . . . beyond what some thought was the final insult to the Lord God in Heaven above.

Thinke on this. God in Heaven above did create humans with a braine, and with the abilitie to thinke clearelie. In addition, He did allow us to have free will, to make our owne choices in life.

Doo we not faithfullie praie to Him everie daie and ask Him to blesse us with wisedome? Thinkest thou that He heareth not our humble praiers? Or, woorse, that He heareth and answereth not?

He did bestowe upon us all of the greate and wondrous gifts of life, braine, minde, and free will. Thinkest thou that He would want us *not* to use those verie gifts? Thinkest thou that He would desire to keepe us in ignorance? 'Tis follie beyond absurditie to thinke that.

Thinke of thy childe. An thou hast no childe, imagine how thou wouldst thinke and feele about a childe an thou hadst one.

Wouldst thou wish thy childe *not* to thinke? Nay. Nay. 'Twould be thy naturall desire to see thy childe, ech daie, goe beyond where he had beene the daie before . . . beyond what she had thought a fortnight agoe.

'Tis my fervent beleefe and faithe that the wondrous Lord God in Heaven above taketh delight ech and everie time anie man, woman, or childe advanceth the knoweledge of science. Alwaies remember, we are His children. God loveth us. He is proud of us everie time we goe beyond where we have beene.

✻ ✻ ✻ ✻ ✻ ✻

List whilst I tell thee how we, thou and I, shall goe beyond where others have gone in the studie of life. We shall learne together how and why humans doo what we doo. We shall studie how to improve life . . . thy life, and life for all humanitie.

Wouldst thou wish to feele better? Wouldst like to knowe what to eate, soe that thou mightst live longer, healthier, and happier? Thy minde can be made more wise and better able to thinke. Art interested? Dost thou e'er woonder how to cure thine ills?

I can help thee. Prithee forgive me an I seeme immodest. I doo moste sincerelie beleeve that thou hast the right to knowe whence commeth mine information.

I am a phisition, philosopher, scientist, and logician. I have doone muche researche in laboratories, in universities, and among the folke in manie shires in our countrie.

Few have looked into the science of what causeth what on this planet Earth, and in the heavens above. Correlation 'tween two events doth not necessarilie meane that either did cause the other. Else, one could reache the conclusion that the crowe of the cock causeth the sunne to rise.

I doo sincerelie hope thou hast the wisedome and goode common sense to keepe ope thy minde as thou readest *BEYOND BEYOND BEYOND*. Then, and onelie then, shalt thou be able at leaste to consider my thoughts, which I have gathered from yeeres of studie, discourse, and thinking.

It paineth me to knowe that cleare thinking and education doo not necessarilie goe togither. Frequentlie it e'en appeareth that the verie opposite is true.

Verilie, thou shouldst have thy dubiosities. Howe'er, thou must ne'er close thy minde to alternate possibilities in thy life.

❋ ❋ ❋ ❋ ❋ ❋

And now, prepare thy selfe to goe to a world beyond where others have beene.

Doo, prithee, enjoie my cogitations. I hope they are beneficiall to thee.

Chapter 2

Whither Goest Thou?

Centre thy selfe

Dost thou oft finde thy selfe at odds with others? Art thou at the end, whilst others occupie the centremoste place? Dost thou feel off of centre?

Or, maihap, thou didst juste beginne, whilst others are beyond.

The centre is where all of importancie happeneth.

Centre thy selfe.

Then, there, thou shalt have the moste enjoiement. Life 'twill be woonderfull.

And, strange as it maie seeme, 'twill gaine thee the greatest riches.

About politicks and centring

All polititions trie to be in the centre. Nay, prithee correct that. All polititions trie *to appeare to be* in the centre. They wish to be perceived as wanting not too much tyrannicall government oppression, nor, else, too much libertie.

I doo not agree with the polititions. Centre *thy selfe*. Centre not thine ideas. Be not moderate in ideas. Rather, be moste passionate in thy beleefes, in life, in ideas, in studie, for libertie, in worke, in love, &c.

Be centred onelie in thy selfe. But be sure to doo that.

Ground thy selfe

An thou art centred, 'tis a new concept also to be grounded. Flie not awaie from important events in thy life. Face thy troubles directlie. Grounding thy selfe is extremelie important. 'Tis second in importancie onelie to being centred.

Elevate thy selfe

Be free of cares. Learne to flie (in thine imagination onelie. Doo not, of course, jump off of a building.). Take not thy life too seriouslie. Life 'tis to be enjoied.

Be spirituall

Some concentrate onelie on material goodes and pleasures. Ope thy hart and minde to the spirituall. Be not locked into Earth and foode and little else.

Thinke beyond thine owne life and worke . . . e'en beyond thy familie . . . beyond thy shire . . . beyond thy countrie . . . beyond Earth.

Muse oft whence we came, where we have beene, and, of moste importancie, *why*. All waies thinke on why.

Place thy feete firmlie in realitie

Be not sweeped awaie from realitie. Waste not thy valuable time and life by cogitations on things and ideas that are not real. Existence, and not appearance, is what should occupie thy minde and bodie and life.

Be at all times a philosopher

Thinke.

Chapter 3

BEYOND

An thou hast read this far, thou art beyond in minde and theorie where moste human beings e'er finde them selves. Far beyond. Far, far beyond.

Goode.

Wondrous.

Since thou hast learned to addresse life beyond what others can doo, thou art readie to venture foorth.

Thou art readie to give application to what we have learned.

Verilie, thou art prepared to go beyond beyond.

PART II

BEYOND

BEYOND

Chapter 4

The Wisedome of Being Healthie

Now that thou art beyond beyond, thou must learne to improve thy bodie and thy minde. That knoweledge, *and putting it to use*, are part of wisedome.

There are foure maine parts to the wisedome of being healthie, to wit:

- Eate goode foode.
- Exercitation of thy bodie.
- Get enough sleepe.
- Thinke thee well.

Ech is important enough to have a chapter unto its selfe.

Chapter 5

Eate Goode Foode

Avoid fattie foodes

Instruction: Avoid fattie foods, such as the red meate of animals and the rich yellow part of milk from cows, which is the creame.

Explanation: Although some phisition freends disagree, I bethinke me that such fattie foode and drinke clog thine arteries within thy bodie. That sloweth the flowe of bloud from the hart to the braine. With less bloud flowing through the braine, the braine sloweth in the function which it doth, which is thinking. With slowed thinking, thou shalt be stupid.

Conclusion: Avoid too muche fattie foodes. Else thou shalt become stupid.

Eate more fruits and vegetables

Instruction: Feede more fruits and vegetables to thy familie. 'Twill make all of ye happie and healthie.

Explanation: Animals roame and wander afar. Fruits and vegetables staie in one place as they growe and develop.

Conclusion: Everie one in thy familie should eate more fruits and vegetables. Then thy selfe and thy spouse will staie at home: happie and faithfull. Also, 'twill allow thee to raise thy children to remaine close to the familie after they are married. All of this, in turn, will stop diseases from coming into thy home.

Eate not too muche salt

Instruction: More than enough salt is more than enough salt.

Explanation: Salt is a crystal which melteth within thy bodie. As it melteth, it causeth thy bloud to become hotter. With hotter bloud, 'twill flowe through thine arteries too fast. That will cause thy hart to worke harder. That, in turn, will cause danger to thy hart, to thy healthe, and to thy life.

Conclusion: Be goode to thy hart: eate lesse salt.

Eate not too much sweete foode

Instruction: Too muche cakes and sugars are not goode for thee.

Explanation: Mine empiricall observation is that those who eate a lot of cakes and sugars are fatt. Applieng logick, I woondered: Could being fatt make one eate more cakes and sugars? Nay. That doth not make sense. Ergo, it muste be that the eating of the cakes and sugars is the cause, and becoming fatt is the result.

I knowe not why. Surelie, those who eate cakes and sugars doo soe insteade of eating a like amount of fruits and vegetables. Maihap 'tis as simple as that there are things in fruits and vegetables that make one thinne. Cakes and sugars doo not conteine that thinning ingredient.

Conclusion: An thou eatest too muche cakes and sugars, thou shalt be fatt.

Conclusion

None can see the future.

Howe'er, some daie, far in the future, folke will looke back and see that the strange phisition philosopher Shillaber

Montabue saide in the 16th centurie what most phisitions thought was just plaine follie, to wit:

- Avoid fattie foodes.
- Eate more fruits and vegetables.
- Eate not a lot of salt.
- Eate not too much sweete foode.

Oh, ye in the future, would that there were a waie that I could knowe todaie whether future science will proove me right on these health advices.

Chapter 6

Exercitation of Thy Bodie

Goe foorth and walk. Doo soe several times ech and everie weeke. 'Tis goode for thee. After thou art able to walk fast and well, maihap thou mightst trie to runne. An thou runnest, thou wouldst have to spend lesse time than an thou choosest to walk for thine exercitation.

Plaie a game. Plaieng is goode for thee in manie waies. 'Tis fun, and it usuallie bringeth exercitation to thy minde as well as to thy bodie.

Doo all of this in the fresh aire.

When thou exercisest on a reguler schedule, at leaste thrice ech weeke, 'twill make thee muche healthier.

The exercitation shouldeth make thee breathe more, taking in more aire. But doo not breathe too muche more.

Finde a freend or some freends with whome to doo thine exercitation. 'Twill be more enjoiable.

Mine empiricall observation is that those who have exercitation at leaste thrice ech weeke are happier, healthier, and live longer. Of these observations I am sure.

I shall attempt to explaine why. I am lesse sure of the explanation of why than am I of the fact that regular exercitation is goode for thee—verie goode for thee. Prithee refer to my chapters on science to understand how I can be sure of *what*, whilst I maie not be as sure of *why*.

It is certeine that exercitation maketh thy hart beate faster during the walk or run or game. Howe'er, 'tis my beleefe that, when an exercitationer is not at the moment exercising, the hart beate sloweth to a slower rate than an thou didst no exercitation.

We are still on mine unproven theorie as to why those who exercise live happier, healthier, and longer.

With a generallie slower hart beate, it alloweth thy hart to handle more work *or plaie* when under stresse.

With that increased strength and capabilitie of the hart, 'tis easier for thee to "give thy hart awaie." That is, thou canst become in love more easilie. Further more, when thou art in love, thou shalt be a better lover than one of slouthe.

Goode love will make thee happier. An thou art happier, thou shalt be healthier. An thou art happier and healthier, thou shalt live longer.

In conclusion, to fall in love, and to live happier and healthier, goe foorth and walk.

Chapter 7

Get Enough Sleepe

Hast thou e'er had an insufficiencie of sleepe, and felt verie tired, wearie, exhausted, drained, and without strength? *And*, hast thou e'er had enough sleepe, felt fullie rested, and experienced the joie and woonder of going about thy life rejoicinglie?

Remember well those two feelings. Thinke throughlie of them. Thinke againe of them.

Which did feele better? Aye, thou sayest that being fullie rested felt far, far better than being exhausted.

Deare reader, 'tis that simple. Thou needest not an other word to explaine the third part of the wisedome. It can be simplie stated in three words: Get enough sleepe.

Chapter 8

Thinke Thee Well

Moste oft for humour, on occasion for sarcasm, and rarelie to teach a lesson, a *sperling* will be spoken or writ. 'Tis a single use of words to conveie two meanings bothe at the same time.

I knowe not for certeine whence commeth the word. I researched it at the librarie at the universitie. I was unable to finde the sourse. Nay, I could not e'en finde the word at all.

I recall that, as a childe, my grandfather saide sperlings oft. He was a clever scholar. He tolde me that sperlings were named after a smart and verie wittie court jester named Sperling, in the 12th centurie.

I knowe not whether to beleeve that. Grandfather was probablie jesting with me. Else the librarie filled with bookes would at the leaste have the word in some booke.

Grandfather was the onelie person I have e'er knowne who was able to saie sperlings excellent well. Few saie them at all, and verie few saie them well. Maihap there is not a word in our language to describe such plaieng with words. Soe, untill I knowe more, I bethinke me that I shall continue to call it a *sperling*.

Is't not of interest how important words are? An I knowe the word for an idea, I can expresse it in one word. When I knowe not the word, I must write manie words to explaine to thee that I knowe not the one word.

✳ ✳ ✳ ✳ ✳ ✳

The title of this chapter is "Thinke Thee Well." 'Tis a sperling. One meaning is that thou canst learne how to thinke in goode measure and to be smart about it. The second meaning is that, an thou art sicke, thou canst thinke thy self well, and hence become well. Thy minde can doo that for thee.

✳ ✳ ✳ ✳ ✳ ✳

The first meaning is that thou shouldst learne to thinke well. Practice with the use of thy minde.

Thinke thou. Hast thou ne'er dismissed an idea ere 'twas e'en seriouslie considered?

Surelie thou wouldst not wish to doo soe againe.

Prithee, for thine owne sake, thinke.

- Ope thy minde
- Have thy dubiosities.
- Consider carefullie.
- Be not stupidlie stubborn.
- Exercise thy wit.
- Be of goode humour.
- Thinke.

✳ ✳ ✳ ✳ ✳ ✳

The second meaning is that, an thou art sicke, thou canst thinke thee well. Thinke thee goode thoughts. In manie cases, that will make thee well, or soe manie beleeve.

Manie phisitions and scientists saie 'tis a placebo. That meaneth that, although it hath no medicinal effects, thine act of thinking throughlie that thou shalt be well will of its selfe make thee well. Some beleeve that the hearbes one taketh for a sickenesse are purelie placeboes. Verilie, they doo seeme to worke.

'Tis unpossible at this time to give assurance whether 'tis the hearbes or the beleefe of the sicke person. We neede more studies on this subject.

I am confident that future science will shew that the placebo its selfe can in fact make one well, in some cases, without an other medicine.

Here, as in other parts of life, thou muste choose without knowing for sure an 'tis right. Thou hast naught to lose by trieng.

In conclusion of this part, an thou art sicke, in addition to all that the phisition doth, thinke thee well.

Chapter 9

BEYOND BEYOND

Thou hast ventured beyond where moste humans have thought of going. . . . Beyond e'en what they knowe existeth. . . .

Beyond what they can, e'en in their moste imaginative dreames, imagine.

Thy minde and bodie are in tune, one with the other.

Thou hast gotten thy selfe centred, grounded, and elevated. Thou art spirituall, and thou art fullie in realitie. Thou art a philosopher who will all waies thinke.

Thou hast absorbed the wisedome of being healthie. Thou knowest well the four maine parts of that wisedome.

Thou hast allowed thy minde to wander beyond. . . .

Thou hast allowed thy minde to woonder beyond. . . .

Aye, and verilie, e'en beyond that, to beyond beyond.

Art thou readie for the next step?

Darest thou e'en contemplate what might lie beyond where thou now art?

Dare to thinke it.

Aye, dare to thinke it.

Dare to do it.

Dare to go beyond beyond beyond.

The verie next part of this booke explaineth a bit about science. 'Tis necessarie knoweledge ere thou art trulie prepared to go beyond beyond beyond.

Prithee studie well the chapters on science.

Then, dare to venture beyond beyond beyond.

PART III

SCIENCE

Chapter 10

Science: Logick, Theorie, or Empiricall Observation?

There hath beene a lot of arguement about what is goode science. Should we use logick, or theorie, or empiricall observation?

Some saie 'tis onelie logick that we neede.

Logick 'tis a wondrous studie. It can be part of science. Muche . . . verie muche . . . can be learned therefrom, but onelie an thou beginnest with correct facts. An I were to saie that all humans have nineteene legs, I could then conclude by correct and proper logick that thou, who art a human, hast the verie same number of legs, to wit, nineteene.

Theorie helpeth in verie large measure. Oft, we start with a theorie alone. Then we must test it. An 'twere not tested, the theorie might leade us astraie.

Let us looke to an example. Aristotle, the famous Greeke philosopher, was absolutelie brilliant. He maie be saide to have actuallie invented logick as a course of studie. His wisedome was centuries into the future from his time.

Howe'er, this brilliant logician and theorist named Aristotle did state as fact that men naturallie have more teethe than doo women. All he had to doo was to looke into the mouths of manie men and manie women. Then he could have actuallie counted the teethe. He would have found that men and women have the exact same number of teethe (ere they beginne falling out).

Theories must be tested by *empiricall observation.* We must actuallie looke, observe, and count, ere we can saie with assurance that our theorie is correct.

There are manie empirics in the land who are cousenors. They saie, "Buy my medicine and thou shalt be cured. Ne'er minde what the phisitions saie. Trie it. It worketh."

And the poore folke buy . . . and trie . . . and die.

Alack, the empirics who are cousenors make the folke doubt the whole worthie thought of empiricall observation.

Proper empiricall observation 'tis important to science. Witnesse what the brilliant scholar Aristotle saide about teethe. His logick was wondrous. His theorie about the inside of mouths was certainlie worth looking into. (Forgive me that last bit of dubious humour. 'Tis an other sperling.) But, alas, he did not looke.

Chapter 11

Science: Logick, Theorie, *AND* Empiricall Observation

The brilliant folke who needlesslie and ceaselesslie argue to pick either logick *or* theorie *or* empiricall observation doo muche to slowe the progresse of science. All three are important.

Logick alone is like mathematics alone. Surelie, two plus two added togither will alwaies make four. But of what use is that to anie one excepting a mathematician? Unless we applie it to life, 'tis useless. For use, we must have two *of something* plus two *of something*. Then we shall have four *of something*.

Let us looke at logick alone:

1. All elephants can read bookes and speake.
2. Eleph is an elephant.
3. Therefore, Eleph can read bookes and speake.

That is correct and proper in logick. But, verilie, the elephant Eleph cannot read bookes, nor can he speake (other than making elephant sounds).

Theorie is what moste have relied upon for centuries to obteine knoweledge. Howe'er, as we have seene in the previous chapter, untested theories can be wrong.

Empiricall observation hath come upon the academic world onelie recentlie as a serious studie. And, alas, as happeneth oft, the cousenors come along with the new idea.

Empiricall observation is oft used to proove (or disproove) a theorie.

A verie important use of empiricall observation is as a starting point. The empiricall observation commeth first. Then we reason inductivelie toward a theorie.

After setting foorth the theorie, we must then conduct experiments to test againe.

And what doo we doo when we have made an empiricall observation, have made a theorie as to *what* worketh, but we knowe not *why* it worketh?

I am at such a stage on manie of mine empiricall observations. Let us take just one example.

From observation of manie yeeres, I have learned that manie—*not all*—people who eate large amounts of fattie foodes are stupid. Mine empiricall observation was the first step.

Step two was to formulate a theorie. In formulating the theorie, I applied logick. It hath taken yeeres for me to put this all togither. I shall trie to explaine it breeflie.

Could being stupid cause people to eat large quantities of fattie foodes? Whilst 'tis a possibilitie an I were to applie onelie logick, it doth not make muche common sense.

Applying the verie same logick, but with what seemeth to be more common sense, it seemeth more likelie that the eating of the fattie foodes is the cause, and the being stupid is the effect.

Now we must experiment to test the correctness of this theorie. That may take yeeres. We must also figure out *why* this happeneth.

Now we come to a verie interesting part. I have made the empiricall observations. I have set foorth my theorie. I shall not be sure the theorie is correct untill I test it. An 'tis correct, then I must trie to figure out *why* 'tis correct. All of this 'twill take yeeres. This is unlike the flim-flam of the cousenors, who promise instant miracles. Real knoweledge taketh time to test and learne.

In the meanwhile, what doo we doo in our lives?

Mine answer, for my selfe, and 'tis mine opinone 'twould be goode for thee: doo not eate verie much fattie foodes, or 'twill, *maihap*, make thee stupid.

I did set this foorth, so that thou mightst knowe that the advices I give in the chapter "Eate Goode Foode" have a goode foundation in empiricall evidence. I am quite certeine, for example, that eating large quantities of fattie foodes correlateth muche with being stupid.

Howe'er, I have not worked out nor tested the theorie sufficientlie to call it a scientific fact.

Mine explanation as to the causing agent is still a bit of conjecture. The *why* I am less certeine of. Howe'er, the correlation of eating fattie foodes and stupiditie is certeine.

Soe, thou canst see that using logick, theorie, and empiricall observation, I have come up with a theorie which probablie will make thy life longer and more enjoiable. The important word is *probablie*. Alas, we shall ne'er knowe everie thing. Yet, we must make decisions about how to live our lives in the meanwhile.

Untill we knowe more, or untill my theorie be prooven to be false, I suggest stronglie to thee that thou eatest not muche fattie foodes.

Chapter 12

Science and Sex

Thinke not that this chapter will deal with sexual advice. It will not increase thine abilities in bed. Howe'er, maihap 'twill improve all of the relations among the men and women on Earth.

Who is smarter, a man or a woman? Didst thou saie a man? How knowest thou that?

Aye, verilie, men doo hold more positions of importancie in business and education. My professor of philosophie at Oxford Universitie was a woman. She was therefore viewed as being in the wrong place. How could a woman obteine suche a loftie position?

How, indeede. Fie on those who ask. She did obteine hir position by being absolutelie a genius in all of hir studies and teaching. Hir heade was filled with more wisedome than the heades of several men . . . or women.

Women doo differ from men. A simple looke will tell thee that. Further more, women doo beare children. Men doo not.

When it commeth to using the heade to thinke, there is no evidence to showe that men are anie more smart . . . or lesse smart . . . than women.

For me, for my life, one of the greatest joies of which I knowe is to finde a woman with whome I can share my joies, my bed, my thoughts, and my moste secret ideas. Bicause of the fact that women *are not* different from men in the abilitie to thinke, I finde that a woman can be a deare freend. Bicause of the fact that women *are* different from men, I finde that a woman can be my dearest freend.

Maihap the daie will come when men and women can worke and plaie as equalls. No longer will ech pretend that men are smarter and wiser, whilst pretending that women are weake and helplesse. None of those assumptions be true. No longer will ech sex blame the other for not onelie its owne troubles, but for all the troubles on Earth. 'Tis follie for men and women to viewe ech other as enemies. Onelie by working *and plaieng* together can Earth be made a happier, healthier, and safer place for all animals, humans, and plants.

Men are neither smarter nor wiser than women . . . nor lesse smart nor lesse wise. If all would stop pretending in what appeareth to be a game of follie, we all shall be better.

I ask ech of ye: Wouldst thou not be happier an thou couldst speake to thy spouse or lover as an equall, sharing ideas, feelings, and thine innermoste energie? Trie it. Aye, indeede, trie it. What canst thou lose?

PART IV

BEYOND

BEYOND

BEYOND

Chapter 13

Energie

Energie. 'Tis a new word that I derived from Latin and Greeke. Alas, my humilitie leaveth me for juste this verie moment. Prithee forgive me. I am indeede proud. I hope that folke in the future will properlie chronicle that, in 1599, the word *energie* was first introduced into the English language by Shillaber Montabue.

Energie, the same as its Latin and Greeke rootes, meaneth power, worke, capacitie for worke, effort, activitie, strength, e'en passion. Energie can be physical, mental, from thy hart, or spirituall. Energie can be produced by machines, by people, by animals, by the elements (for example, lightning, raine, floode, volcanoes), by spirituall forces, and, I beleeve future generations will learne of more causes of energie.

Language is indeede interesting to studie. Moste words enter our language by chance. They are not precise in meaning. By use, folke learne what ech word meaneth. The usage assigneth the meaning.

That is why I am particularlie pleased to introduce *energie* into the English language. 'Tis fullie formed and, as thou canst readilie see from the above, 'tis precisely defined.

In the verie next chapter, thou shalt learne how to use energie to improve thy life.

Chapter 14

Manifest Thy Selfe

Absorb energie without within

Energie is all around thee. The sunne, starres, moone, rainbowe, thunder, as well as other folke, animals, trees, and grass, all glowe with energie. Absorb all that energie from without thy hart and minde and bodie within thy hart and minde and bodie.

Absorb energie within within

Within thy bodie is energie. Glowe throughlie soe that all parts of thy bodie can absorb the energie from all of the other parts of thy bodie. The same should be doone for energie for thy minde, and for thy hart.

Manifest thy selfe

An thou dost all of the above, thine entire selfe will glowe with energie. Use thine energie to manifest thy selfe. Project thine internal selfe into an external selfe that thy freends may use to absorb thine energie without them selves within them selves. Onelie goode commeth from that.

An thou glowest with energie, an thou manifestest thy selfe, maihap thou shalt be able to take thy freends beyond where they are . . . beyond what they knowe . . . beyond beyond. An thou and they are luckie, thou mightst e'en be able to guide them in to the world beyond beyond beyond.

'Tis a joie to manifest thy selfe and to give thine energie to others: familie, freends, strangers, animals, and plants. An thou glowest with sufficient energie, and thou manifestest thy selfe enough, thou canst e'en give energie back to the sunne.

'Tis an utmoste joie and an uttermoste reward of life to be able to glowe with sufficient energie to manifest thy selfe enough to give energie back to the sunne. When thou dost that . . . when thou hast the experience of giving energie to the universe . . . thou art beyond beyond beyond.

Manifest thy selfe to thine utmoste and uttermoste. Glowe with energie beyond beyond beyond. Recharge the sunne with thine energie.

Chapter 15

BEYOND BEYOND BEYOND

Looke well whither thou hast ascended. Thou art beyond where others have gone or dare to goe. More than having learned to centre thy selfe, &c., thou hast gone beyond that.

Thou hast learned the foure maine secrets of the wisedome of goode healthe.

Thou hast gone beyond that.

Thou thinkest as doth a scientist and a philosopher.

List well, and thinke throughlie of this. Thou hast gone e'en beyond all of the above. Thou hast gone beyond beyond.

Without mine e'en mentioning it, thou knowest as an absolute certeintie that peace is necessarie for the survival of people, animals, plants, and Earth its selfe. Doo prithee teach all the folke of the Earth, and tell them againe and againe, that war is stupid. That is the one obligation which I hope that thou shalt assume, as thou hast gone beyond moste of thy fellowe human beings. Remember well and teach well and oft: *War is stupid.*

Thou hast absorbed the inchantment, inrichment, and vertue of dwelling in the world beyond beyond. The sunne and the starres are thine. Thou art speciall.

Thou hast woondered beyond where others e'en knowe there is a place to woonder. Thou hast beene a witnesse to science beyond where others e'en contemplate. Thou hast looked up and seene the rainebowe after the shewers, whilst others looke onelie down and merelie see the mudde. Thou hast viewed phantasticallie what others viewe as mondeyne. And thou hast doone it all without using anie hurtfull drogges. Thou hast kept thy minde alive and all waies aware.

Thou hast experienced the energie of the fierie marvell of originall thought. Thy bloud and thy bowels flowe smoother than the bloud and bowels of other folke. Thou hast received all of the beneficiall woonders of those who have dared to venture into the world beyond where others either goe or thinke.

Thou hast arrived in the world beyond beyond beyond. Thou art speciall.

Muche luck, love, happinesse, joie, adventure, successe, welth, peace, freedome of thought, freedome of action, prosperitie, knoweledge, and healthe to thee, for now and for all the daies in the future.

All waies, for all of thy daies, fore'er, remember well and throughlie:

THOU ART SPECIALL.

Fare thee well, oh learned freend.

BIBLIOGRAPHIE

BIBLIOGRAPHIE

57

Reginald Scot: *The Discoverie of Witchcraft*, Imprinted at London by William Brome, 1584.

Prithee thinke me not arrogant for listing juste one sourse. See my dedication of this booke, and thou shalt understand the enormous influence Reginald Scot hath had upon my life and my thoughts.

Where I am right, my deare freend Reginald deserveth muche of the credit.

Where I am in errour, I onelie am answerable.

A COURSE IN RENAISSANCE ENGLISH

By
Robert A. Steiner

Background

The language in *BEYOND BEYOND BEYOND* is sufficiently similar to modern English to be understandable. It is sufficiently different to make interesting reading.

Milords and miladies [instead of *ladies and gentlemen.* Notice that *milords* comes first, because they rank higher . . . or so they thought. *Milord* and *miladie* have a short "i," as in *miss.*]:

A study of Renaissance English 102 (the next section), preferably aloud, will increase your enjoyment of *Beyond Beyond Beyond.* To further enhance your experience, you might wish to read the entire book aloud: to yourself, or, even better, to be shared with others.

You can get good experience in the language, and have much fun, by talking with family and friends in Renaissance English. You can enjoy a visit to any of the numerous, wondrous Renaissance Faires around the globe. With a bit of study and practice, this course and book will help you to pass yourself off as a native when you do visit.

Real slowly. Speak slowly. Savor the words and sentences. People of the Renaissance times were not in the fast lane. Remember (dost thou remember?), it was before television, before stereo music, before radio, before telephone, before movies, before computers (aye, ere computer games), before cars, before airplanes, before the harnessing of electricity . . . it was even before the Super Bowl. The only thing resembling a railway car was pulled by horses along wooden rails. It was used primarily for mining.

Compare the speed and urgency (or lack thereof) of their culture with ours. It took them over a century to shorten *thou dooest* to *thou dost.* In our day, the facsimile machine was on the market for only 43 minutes when somebody decided to call it a *fax.* In order to suit our modern fast-paced life style, just 27 minutes after the noun *fax* was coined to describe a facsimile machine, the verb *fax* was born. It means to send a document via a fax (the noun). Just 16 minutes later, some sophisticated business person decided that the word *document* takes too much time to say. After all, it has three syllables. Let's just call it a *fax*. Now I can fax a fax from my fax to your fax in seconds.

In Renaissance times, reading and conversation were two of the primary joys *and forms of entertainment* in life. Conversation, *real conversation*, took place. People communicated with one another *as an end in itself*, not merely as the means to accomplish some other worthy end. They enjoyed the language. With all due respect to Strunk and White* ("Omit needless words. Vigorous writing is concise. A sentence should contain no unnecessary words, a paragraph no unnecessary sentences."), embellishment of the language was a joy.

In the sciences, such as physics and chemistry, rules, by their nature, have no exceptions. In language, rules are general and do have exceptions. Sometimes there are no rules. For example, in the English language of today, there are no rules to tell you how to correctly pronounce the words:

> *bough*
> *cough*
> *dough*
> *rough*.

Today we have comprehensive dictionaries and standardized spelling. Radio, television, telephone, newspapers, and magazines disseminate language and information around the

---

* Strunk, William, Jr., and E. B. White: *The Elements of Style*. New York: Macmillan Publishing Co., Inc. [1959] 1979, 23. *The Elements of Style* is a masterpiece, but it did not sell well in Renaissance times.

world. We have extensive world-wide travel. Even with this virtually instant communication across the globe, regional accents remain. Additionally, there are choices to be made when speaking. Today's scholars differ as to the proper pronunciation of many of today's words; for example, *envelope*, *data*, and *ration*.

In Renaissance times, communication and travel covered much shorter distances. There was not standardized spelling. There were no comprehensive dictionaries. Samuel Johnson's *Dictionary of the English Language*, the first comprehensive English dictionary, was not published until 1755. Without those communication devices, and with far less mobility of people, regional differences tended to be more extreme. No one from that time is alive today to speak to us. We have no recordings. It should therefore come as no surprise that today's scholars specializing in Renaissance English differ as to the pronunciation of some words.

In teaching this course, we had to make choices from the alternative spellings and pronunciations available. For example, in Renaissance English literature, we find *great* spelled *great*, *greate*, *gret*, and *grette*. Similarly, we find *head* spelled *head*, *heade*, *hed*, *hedde*, and *heid*. For simplicity and consistency, we chose the spellings and the inferred pronunciations used by Shillaber Montabue in his writing:

> *greate*, pronounced with a long "a" (as in *made*).
> *heade*, also pronounced with a long "a."

Renaissance English 102 will stand you in good stead. Take your time. Enjoy the language. People of the Renaissance times did.

And now, get thy selfe into the moode to learne a new language and to read a booke that will tickle thy fancie to thine uttermoste desire.

Renaissance
English 102
Fundamentals

To Beginne

Thou is the familiar form of *you*, used with family (by parents to children, not by children to parents), friends, and, alas, when speaking to people of a lower class. *Thou* is also used in praying to God, or to any god that is considered to be a personal god. For all others, use *you*. The plural of *thou* is *ye*. The plural of *you* is also *ye*.

Thou is the subject of the sentence; *thee* is the object. Use *thou* and *thee* the same way as you would use *I* and *me*.

> Thou lovest me. I love thee.

Thy is possessive.

> This is thy booke.

Thine is possessive when followed by a vowel sound. That is also true of *mine*.

> Thine eies are beauteous, oh faire and wondrous damsel Eve.
> How knowest thou that, Adam? Thou art looking at mine apple, not at mine eies.

Thine is also used when it is not followed by a noun (the thing possessed). The same is true of *mine*.

> Is this thy toie? Is this toie thine? Is't thine?
> Aye, this is my toie. Aye, this toie is mine. Aye, 'tis mine.

Telling a person to call you *thou* is an indication of friendship.

> How are you todaie?
> I am well [not *fine*. *Fine* is a measure of purity.].
> Whither go you?
> I am not royaltie. Wherefore callest thou me *you*?

For ease of reading, let us take a short cut in phonetics. The long way would be to write:

> *Efficient* is pronounced "e (as in *he*) - fi' (as in *fill*) - se (as in *see*) - ent (as in *bent*)."

Instead, we shall use { } as a short cut, to mean "as in [*word*]."

> *Efficient* is pronounced "e {he} - fi' {fill} - se {see} - ent {bent}."

Aye means *yes*.

Nay means *no*.

Aye and *nay* are unusual sounds to our modern ears. Each is pronounced with a *diphthong*. You start with one vowel sound and slide into another, all in the same syllable. Examples of diphthongs in today's language are the vowel sounds in *boil*, and *mouse*.

For *aye*, say the word *eye* slowly. The vowel sound slides from "ah" into "ee." Pronounce it a few times, until it sounds good. After you master that, try the same vowel sound in *fie*, *boil*, and *joie*.

For *nay*, say the word *neigh* slowly. The vowel sound slides from "e" {next} into "ee" {see}. Now try the same vowel sound in *saie* and *daie*.

Nay is used to reply to a question. It is also used to mean *and moreover*, to introduce an expression stronger than the one just used. Otherwise, use *no* in conversation.

> Hast thou anie monie?
>
> Nay, I have no monie. I would like, nay, love to have a lot of monie.

Verb endings are similar to what we use today, except for the second and third person singular.

You is used for one person. It takes the same verbs as does the plural *ye* (and as does today's *you*).

Thou generally has verbs ending in "est."

> Thou lookest. Thou findest. Thou fallest in love.

Very common verbs are often shortened.

> Thou art. Thou hast. Thou shalt. Thou dost.

He, she, and *it,* as well as other third-person singular subjects of sentences, generally have verbs ending in "eth."

> He proposeth. She accepteth. It occurreth. The wedding happeneth. Time flieth. Anon, in juste fourteene moneths, they are a happie familie of four, with a sonne and a doughter. Nay, nay, thinke not that. The boie and girl were twinborn.

Here, too, the most common verbs are shortened.

> He is. She hath. It will. The dog doth.

The "est" ending is dropped in an imperative.

> Thinke deeper than the centre of Earth.

An sometimes means *if.*

Cousenage is the act of fraud. *Cousenor* is the one committing the fraud.

Please say *prithee* for *please.* It is short for *I praie of thee.* Prithee go on to Advanced Studie.

❋ ❋ ❋ ❋ ❋ ❋

Advanced Studie

Do you remember the familiar *"I" Before "E" Rule* you were taught in school? Let us take another peek at it.

> I before e,
> Except after c,
> Or when sounded as a,
> As in *neighbor* and *weigh,*
> As well as in *seize* and *either,*
> And *leisure* and *neither.*

If it does not have an "h," do not say "sh" or "zh."

> *Sure* is pronounced "syur" (not "shyur"). It rhymes with *pure.*
>
> *Measure* is pronounced "ma' {make} - zyur."

The combination "ci" is often one complete syllable.

> I shall bet you (never *I'll betcha*) that you already know how to pronounce *efficient.*
>
> *Precious* is pronounced "pre' {press} - se {see} - ous {us}."

Words with "oo" often have an "e" at the end of the syllable. *Goode* rhymes with *foode*.

Words ending in "ing" are pronounced by dropping the final "g." *Having* is pronounced as if it were spelled "havin'."

The "ed" at the end of a word is a separate syllable. *Called* is pronounced as if it were hyphenated: "call-ed."

Words we spell with "y" at the end of the syllable were frequently (but not always) spelled with "ie." Spelling was not standardized. Often in one book, by one author, we find different spellings of the same word.

How do you add "ing" to a word ending in "ie"? (I am certain that very question was foremost in your mind.) Just add "ng" (not "ing"). In present times, *play* becomes *playing*. In Renaissance times, *plaie* becomes *plaieng*.

"Sion" and "tion" are pronounced as follows:

> If you now pronounce it "chen," as in *question*, pronounce it "te-on" (long "e" {he}, long "o" {toe}).
>
> If you now pronounce it "shen," as in *direction* or *session*, pronounce it "se-on" (again, long "e" and long "o").

Pronounce "sch" as "sh," as in *schedule*.

"Ea" is generally pronounced with a long "a" {greate}. Such words include *yea*, *heade* and *treasure*, as well as *breake*, *breade*, and *pleasure*. However, *speake* has the "ea" sound close to the "ea" in our present word *bear*, but slower, with a diphthong. The past tense of *speake* is *spake*, pronounced with a long "a."

"Ai" is also pronounced with a long "a." Said slowly and properly, it is the diphthong sound in *nay*. *Saide* rhymes with *paide*; *againe* rhymes with *raine*. *Faire* rhymes with *mayor*.

An "a" not followed in the same syllable by "i," "y," or "e" is usually pronounced as the "a" in *back*. Such words include *ham*, *can*, *father*, *water*, and *man*.

The "aw" in *law* is the vowel sound in *fought, not, Lord, hot*, and *spot*.

OK or *okay* is *not* okay as a Renaissance word. Its use will brand you as an impostor.

> *Okay* indeede. Fie on thee, vile knave. Thinkest thou that thy strange tung and thine evil words will deceive us poore peasants? A plague on thee. Onelie the divell could have sent thee hither to take our monie for thy flim-flam. Take thy selfe and thine *okay* and begone from my shire, ere I separate thy heade from thy bodie. Fie. Fie. Wicked cousenor.

And the gentle people of Renaissance times had no use for impostors.

Those good folk knew how to tell someone off. Unlike today, when we tell a person off in two one-syllable words, or at most three one-syllable words, angry words back then bore the mark of skilled wordsmiths.

Embellish your flattery. (In play mode only) elaborate on your abusive language, without using today's infamous "four-letter words." You will experience the joy of conversation in Renaissance times.

Wouldst like to knowe whither to goe?

> From this place = *hence.*
> From that place = *thence.*
> From what place = *whence.*
> To this place = *hither.*
> To that place = *thither.*
> To what place = *whither.*
>
> To buy a fence, hence goe thither.
> Whither?
> The fence shoppe, of course.
> May I borrow thy horsse?
>
> Aye. Then return hither thence.
> Whence?
> The fence shoppe, or course.
> Where is thy horsse?

I hope the Poetic Licensing Board does not revoke my license for the above.

The above words may also refer to ideas, as well as to physical locations. For example, *whence* may also mean "from what cause or source, from which."

> She mixed two parts of hydrogen and one part of oxygen, whence she got water.
>
> Whence commeth that knoweledge? Further more, I knowe not the words *hydrogen* and *oxygen*. Art thou from the future? Whither takest thou me with these unknowne words, whencesoe'er they came? Wherefore [why, for what reason] layest thou upon my humble heade words beyond my ken?

An thou wouldst juste remaine with me a bit more, thou shalt be graduated from our little school.

❋ ❋ ❋ ❋ ❋ ❋

Graduation

Greetings:

> Goode morrow, milord. [Good morning, my lord.]
> I shall see thee on the morrow [tomorrow].
> God thee goode den, miladie. [May God give you a good day, my lady.]
> Fare ye well, good gentles.

Sir rhymes with *far*. *Goode sir* is a friendly greeting. *Sir* said in a rough tone, without a friendly modifier, is an insult.

The contractions used were different from those we use today.

> Do not say: *don't can't*, and *it's*.
> Do say: *'tis* and *'twould*.
> Instead of *it isn't*, say *'tis not*.

Frequently "v" was omitted, sometimes in writing, and more often in speech.

> 'Twould ne'er doo to say the "v" in *howe'er*.

Long usage of a contraction eventually may allow the apostrophe ['] to be omitted. *Halloween* is short for *All Hallow Even*.

Brace yourself for a mnemonic device. It will help avoid two traps folk learning Renaissance English often fall into. You have all heard of the tax preparers H & R Block. People in Renaissance England did not have an "h" and "r" block. The "h" was not blocked.

> *'Enry 'Iggins* is 'ow 'e 'as to say it, as 'e 'olds 'is ale in 'is 'and.
>
> That is Cockney, and came much later. Renaissance English has the beginning "h" pronounced, except, of course, in *honour* and *hour*.

The "r" was not blocked.

> Unlike today's "Mahk will pahk the cah," the folks in Renaissance England pronounced the "r" rather strongly.
>
> Mark will . . . tie the horsse to the poste.

Words with "ou" and "ow" have a diphthong:

The sound {sah-oond} of *round* {rah-oond} is bound {bah-oond} around {uh-rah-oond} the clown {clah-oon} in the house {hah-oos}. Thou {thah-oo} knowest it well.

"E" at the end of a syllable generally means there is a long vowel sound in the syllable:

> "A" as in *game* and *againe*.
> "E" as in *complete* and *feete*.
> "I" as in *mine* and *finde*.
> "O" as in *toe* and *goe*.
> The long "u" sound is either:
> "oo" as in *flute* and *doore*, or
> "yoo," as in *pure* and *viewe*.

Generally when "u" stands alone in a syllable, it is pronounced "oo."

> Thy cup {coop} runneth {roon'-eth} o'er. Prithee put {poot} it down o'er there ere thy hostesse upbraideth {oop-bray'-deth} thee.

When a "u" syllable has "e" at the end, there are two options available.

"Yoo" as in *cue, cute, mute, pure,* and *sure* (remember - no "sh" sound).
"Oo," as in *flute, rue,* and *runne.*
For *due,* take your choice: "doo" or "dyoo."

The next change in our language is so recent that many of you reading this will remember being taught as a child to say *I shall.* We conjugate the verb as follows:

For normal speech:

I shall
Thou shalt
You will
He, she, it will
We shall
Ye will
They will.

For a stronger statement, for determination, or for a command, we have the strange instruction to change *shall* to *will* and *will* to *shall.* Prithee understand, I do not make the rules; I am simply a humble chronicler:

I *will*
Thou *shalt* (no change here. Sometimes it will be *thou wilt.*)
You *shall*
He, she, it *shall*
We *will*
Ye *shall*
They *shall*
I *will* beat him in tennis, and he *shall* pay me the amount we have bet on the game.

Sometimes a noun is followed by its pronoun; then comes the verb.

That usage 'tis easie to understand.
This booke 'twill showe thee.

In a question, sometimes *thou* is implied, rather than stated.

Art thou readie? *or* Art readie?

Didst thou saie *Aye*?

Excellent well. An thou art readie, I bid thee a pleasant journie into the world beyond beyond beyond.

ADDENDA

ABOUT THE AUTHORS

For information about Shillaber Montabue, please see the Foreword.

Any subject, any era, any country is likely to challenge the investigative curiosity of Robert A. Steiner. A public speaker, consultant, and entertainer, he has given presentations to universities, law enforcement seminars, and medical and scientific conventions. The eight books he has written include:

MOMMY AND DADDY HAVE SEPARATED:
A Primer for Children

DON'T GET TAKEN! Bunco and Bunkum
Exposed—How to Protect Yourself.

For information about presentations by Robert A. Steiner, please write to:

Wide-Awake Books
Box 659
El Cerrito, CA 94530

Please send:

_____ copies of *DON'T GET TAKEN!* @ $14.95 $_________

_____ copies of *BEYOND BEYOND BEYOND* @ $9.95 $_________

Subtotal $_________

California residents please add sales tax $_________

Postage and handling:
$2 for one book; $4 for two or more books $_________

Total $_________

Send check or money order to:

Wide-Awake Books
Box 659
El Cerrito, CA 94530

Name ____

Address ____

City__________________ State ______ Zip __________

41

For information about presentations by Robert A. Steiner, please write to:

Wide-Awake Books
Box 659
El Cerrito, CA 94530

Please send:

____ copies of *DON'T GET TAKEN!* @ $14.95 $________

____ copies of *BEYOND BEYOND BEYOND* @ $9.95 $________

Subtotal $________

California residents please add sales tax $________

Postage and handling:
$2 for one book; $4 for two or more books $________

Total $________

Send check or money order to:

Wide-Awake Books
Box 659
El Cerrito, CA 94530

Name ____

Address ____

City________________ State ______ Zip __________

41